Manca Macuh

What It Takes to Change Your Life

And How to Actually Make it Work

There comes a time in some people's lives when they see through the fog of their upbringing, through the norms of society, and through the habits, they have been taught to imitate. When the life they thought they wanted turns out to be but a meager reflection of someone else's dream. Finishing school, getting married, buying a house, paying the mortgage, raising a family, going to work day in and day out, and finally retiring, seems to be the road to a happy existence. Granted, this kind of life profoundly agrees with some people, and they love their 9-5 job and the so-called normal way of living is exactly what they had hoped for.

Whether you long for the "normal" or not so normal, if you are reading this, then the ground under your derrière has most probably been profoundly shaken with a realization that you haven't actually been living, but following some internal commandment, that is not in accordance with who you are. You might have even started searching what the heck it is you can do about it before you got hold of this fine book. The life you have been living up till now probably seems like an ever-tightening shell and you are more than ready to hatch into a new beginning. And may I say – although it might be extremely uncomfortable – **good for you.**

A new beginning means stepping forward into the unknown. It doesn't have to be something significant, just new enough that you have little to no experience and no one guiding you through each step. It's dark and probably fills you with a certain degree of excitement, mixed with an adequate amount of dread. Can it be done? Will you make it? Will you end up with nothing? There are the rare individuals who just go for it, following their instincts and courageously stepping in the direction their dreams beckon, letting nothing and no one stand in their way. But the majority of us – although longing for freedom to live as we please – meet actually getting there successfully, with a big fat question mark. It might look something like a deep yearning mixed with underlying angst, and a chill that creeps down your spine when you think of taking the first step. Being afraid of the consequences, fearing success just could not be possible for the likes of you is a common enough stance. For most of us, beginning anew looks something like being thrown into a hurricane of racing thoughts and overwhelming emotions, to the point where we are exhausted before we even give it a go. But it doesn't have to be like that.

The kinds of books like this one, usually fall into the hands of people who have come to find their everyday life to be less and less tolerable and perhaps even unbearable. People who know giving something else a shot is their only hope of filling the emptiness they feel daily. They just know the time for change has come and must be acted upon, not wasted. So if you find yourself to be that person, then **welcome to the rest of your magnificent life.** It's probably not going to unfold the way you may have imagined it would, it might even be difficult at times, but I promise, it's going to be so much more than you could have hoped for. If only you put the time and energy into getting the momentum going. I'm here to help you figure out how to make it work rather sooner than later.

Taking the reins of your life into your own hands is far from a comfortable thing. Not because it's so impossibly difficult, but because most of us are not accustomed to navigating our lives on our own. We don't know how to, because no one had taught us. **Most of us have been taught to simply copy and obey** and that's what we end up doing far beyond our childhood submissiveness. Sadly, many of us don't even know living exactly the way we want to is an option. We have been told to be good and do what we are told, in order to be accepted and loved. And this usually enabled us to survive, but not really thrive to our fullest. We are still frequently told to stop dreaming, to be "realistic" instead of being encouraged to let our imagination run wild and create something magical.

The majority of us don't realize that **we are actually allowed to live as we choose**, without having to make sure everyone around us is fine with it. We haven't a clue that this is our given birthright. If we were lucky, we might have been encouraged to try new things as children, but failing was probably often met by some degree of punishment or exclusion. So no wonder even the thought of trying something new is often immersed in deep fear. We imagine that by failing, we could still be punished by society, our family, God, or any other form of authority we have been taught to answer to. We have a hard time believing this life is indeed ours and that we get to say what goes and what doesn't. We don't get to say what others should do, but we sure as heck do when it comes to us and our own choices. **It's called freedom.**

Not feeling free and being scared of not having all the knowledge and experience we think we should have, most of us seek answers from others and feel safer when we are told what to do. Especially in situations that seem new and overwhelming. We might not like being told what to do when we're comfortable, but when we are not or when we are scared even, it often feels safer. It is not often that we are encouraged to look inside of ourselves for answers, being made to feel our own judgment is not to be trusted.

If others tell us exactly what to do, there might also be a possibility of escaping the awful burden of responsibility if something should happen to go wrong. We usually equate being responsible with feeling guilty and guilt is excruciatingly painful. Some people in this world would rather die than stand up for themselves, not being prepared to face the guilt or shame others might bestow upon them. Most of us don't want to carry the burden of upsetting the people we love, dragging their tears and anger like a ball and chain behind us for the rest of our days. We are reluctant to take responsibility for our actions, for our own life, or for our own happiness. As well as not being able to see that how other people feel, react and take care (or not) of themselves and their own happiness is their responsibility alone. **Once we realize our life is our own responsibility, we can start taking steps towards making it a better one.**

The fear of making mistakes is a huge hurdle we are often faced with. In our society, it is frowned upon to make mistakes. In school, you got bad grades for it and at home, you might have gotten scolded or even worse. What if you were to recognize that making mistakes is actually extremely beneficial to your development? What if you saw that through trial and error lies your way to success and that it can be achieved in no other way? What if this game of falling and getting back up could become light and playful? Well, building the life of your dreams can be playful and even fun, **provided you are willing to look at failures as a necessary part of the journey.**

Though making a mistake can be accompanied by frustration, of course, it needn't be the reason to give up and feel as if you have failed. To fail is to stop trying altogether. Mistakes might be the very fuel that makes you try again and again until you succeed. Falling and then picking yourself back up builds character, patience, resilience, and self-trust.

The kind of journey where you allow yourself to make mistakes can be an exploration of what is possible. And you don't have to be anxious doing it either. It is possible to calm your mind in the process to make it a favourable companion along your way. Yes, there are things to know in advance. Yes, there are tools to be acquired and experiences to be had. But this can be done, without the dread of your whole world collapsing if at first, you don't succeed. And you probably won't the first time you try. If you do, luck had probably something to do with it.

Another aspect that keeps us stuck and which makes many people give up on their dreams is being absolutely positive they don't have what it takes. The "not me" belief is growing close to an epidemic. Many people don't even try, because the belief of actually being capable of doing something meaningful is so foreign to them. If only they were willing to look at their beliefs, replacing the ones that no longer serve them with more useful ones. I know that anyone – and I mean absolutely anyone – can end up creating the life they dreamed of. The way to begin is by **giving it a chance and taking small steps towards it, saying no to anything that won't bring you there.** It is not a matter of being able to, but of willing to.

The two most difficult challenges we are usually faced with are our own thoughts on the one hand and other people's opinions on the other. I have been told many times that it wasn't normal to want to live the way I had always dreamed of, just because it was something completely different from what people imagined a normal life should look like. At first, I used to believe others knew better, and I believed I was just an odd creature, wishing for something that wasn't acceptable.

But once I realized **we ourselves decide what is acceptable for us,** I started researching a little what other people of similar longings to mine did to have the life I was dreaming of. I learned to keep a low profile and keep my dreams to myself if I didn't want to spend the majority of my time defending them. At first, I imagined that this would somehow isolate me, but in fact, it just gave me the chance to work on my dreams without interruptions, while the people close to me kept their peace of mind, not worrying and not giving me a hard time.

1.
QUITTING THE WAITING GAME

"I am not a product of my circumstances. I am a product of my decisions"

Stephen Covey

For you to move ahead smoothly, you need first to be clear on what it is you really want and who it is you want to become. To get down to the core of what you truly want, it is important to find out what your true self desires. It is also vital that you become completely honest with yourself, which doesn't come naturally to most people. **Being honest with yourself entails getting to know who you are and what your weaknesses are, as well as your strengths.** It means peeling off all that is false, all that you have borrowed from others, thinking it to be your own. All that your parents, society, the media, your friends, and other significant people have helped create by letting you know how you should be and especially how you shouldn't.

Living your truth could mean going against your family's values, your friends' opinions, your partner's expectations, and so on. Being afraid of loss can be so scary, that we stick with what we've got and stay where we are, living in a perpetual cycle of deceit, wishing for something to happen outside of us which would bring better circumstances to let us thrive. **Wishing for your life to get better will not get you there. Acting on it will.** And yes, this may bring about some loss, but you gain so much more in the end.

Waiting for someone or something to take away your woes and struggles may require a lifetime. So why not do it yourself? I guarantee you that by starting, something happens to point you in the right direction. Be it an idea, something you hear, see, someone you meet, etc. I have always found it to be the case, **that when you make a move, the Universe makes one too.** And if you stick with taking small steps, are willing to learn from your mistakes, and get back on your feet over and over again, this brings so many opportunities, you won't know what to do with.

Now sticking to it is the tricky part. Many people stop after they fall a couple of times, thinking it to be too difficult. Being so used to instant gratification, we have forgotten that life just doesn't work that way. The laws of the Universe state that **for you to get the things you want, you have to become the person these things are matched with.** Many people are put off by the mere thought of changing who they are to become a better version of themselves. It makes them feel they aren't good enough as they are as well as being afraid of change. But that is not the point here. You are not changing who you are on the inside, you are simply changing your armour. You are building a more sustainable version of yourself that is capable of handling change, dealing with your emotions, and navigating your life. That is all.

Have you ever heard of the saying "God helps those who help themselves"? Some people pray to God every day to make their life better, to make their suffering easier. Yet they hardly do anything about it actively themselves. They sit around waiting for something to happen, doing absolutely nothing to even get close to their desired goal or to move out of their predicament. What this saying is trying to teach is, that **in order for things to become easier, you need to keep taking action**. This means putting in the work, not overdoing it, and always taking the next step. And then things start opening up. They get easier, new opportunities come, help comes in different forms and results start piling up.

It's funny how things always seem to work out whenever we manage to focus on the job at hand. **Whatever we focus on, grows.** This is not a theory, it is fact. If we focus on the things that are in our way, they will seem to get bigger and bigger, until we see nothing else, but the enormous mountain of problems we are supposed to be solving. We might try to ignore them by procrastinating, playing video games, watching TV, scrolling on social media, and any other thing we can think of that will deter our minds from the mountain we are supposed to be climbing.

Waiting can make us scared or at least very frustrated, as we expect someone else to get a bulldozer to move the freaking mountain for us. But no one comes. There is no bulldozer as there never was a mountain in the first place, just many things piling up in our head. As we spend so much time thinking of all the things we should have done or should be doing, it starts to become overwhelming and our mind tries its best to suppress our emotions to keep us afloat. But the body knows. By suppressing our emotions, we become tense, anxious, or perhaps even depressed.

Our body is a fantastic indicator of what is happening within us. If we learn to listen to it, we will see what it is that we are trying to suppress. It will inevitably let us know if we have strayed from our true calling, be it by unease or disease. The thing that this huge mountain we think we have to overcome is made of, are scary thoughts and unfelt emotions. But once your start making your way slowly through the fog of fear, it suddenly lifts, revealing to you what must be done next. And everything starts to look manageable. Somehow you start seeing that it's not as impossible as you imagined it to be, but that you can make it happen without being superhuman. Although you may have to get better at certain things as you go, this doesn't have to happen all at once and you don't have to know everything before you even begin. Getting better at things will come on its own if you just keep going, allowing yourself to make mistakes and learning from them.

So don't waste your time waiting. Just make a plan and roughly stick to it, picking yourself up when you stumble. Results will come, and so will opportunities. By taking action the way will become clearer and clearer and the answers you might need will appear as you go. The effort you put in gets the energy going. Life isn't just things happening one after the other randomly, it's energy changing from one form to another, moving in a pattern that might not be clear to us. It just might take a bit of time for the results to come back to you, but they do eventually. If you do nothing or keep on doing what you have always been doing, you will get that mirrored back to you and things will stay the same, as the same old pattern is being created over and over. **When you get stuck, try something different,** even if you're not sure if it's the right thing to do or the right way to go. This is the only way to get experience and get it right in the end, should things not work out the first time.

Become an assistant to your life. How? Well, you will need a different mindset. You will need to **start focusing on solutions instead of problems**. You will need to build up the power to believe in a positive outcome even at times when it seems as if everything is against you. Because it isn't. Things turning into seeming chaos means something is shifting. There is always chaos before change, that is a fact of life. You need to become your biggest cheerleader, your biggest fan, your biggest support. Just do the next thing that needs to be done, and don't stop until you succeed.

With that being said, there is a time to stop and wait, especially when you are emotional which inevitably prevents you from seeing things clearly. Sometimes you might need to think about things thoroughly and taking action might not be the right thing to do. There is a difference between passively waiting for things to change on the outside (which you usually have little to no control over) and taking the time to clear your thoughts to adjust your plan. Waiting can be part of the creative process because answers may not come because of fear, doubt, or mistakes that need to be pondered on.

I know that change is scary and that you might have no idea what's waiting for you in the future, but **the scariest part is what is running through your mind, not what's actually out there.** So waiting to be ready or waiting for things to get easier will only take away years of your precious life. When we are very young, we tend to think we have all the time in the world, but when we enter our thirties or forties, the realization of »now or never« can give us a massive wake-up call. You most certainly can spend all of your life just trotting along blissfully, not having anything special you'd want to change, but if you feel like you do, now is the time to do it, regardless of your age.

Procrastination is something we are all faced with at some point in our lives and unless self-discipline has been instilled in you in early childhood, you too might be struggling to get things done. It usually starts by having thoughts that make up a story of hardship and difficulty, ending in failure. **Procrastination is the result of fear and other unwanted emotions.** It is fueled by the need to escape from the possibility of an unfavorable outcome. On the one hand, we are afraid of what lies ahead, and on the other, we may feel guilt or shame about not doing what we know needs to be done.

Being stuck in a cycle of fear and shame breeds things like depression, feelings of being worthless, being less than, and the like. But the fact is, you are none of those things. **Not being able to do everything at once, doesn't mean you can't do one small thing at a time.** We often forget that imagining a positive outcome and visualization is work too. Because it may seem like a game, it is sometimes overlooked as not important. But it is very important. Little things are the ones that make the whole picture and imagination is a blueprint of how these things will be put together.

So if you feel as if you are unable to move forward, if you think you need to wait for a miracle to happen that will open the doors to a better life, you might want to reevaluate your thoughts. The right time to start a different life just might be right now, regardless of how capable you feel you are at the moment. You can never know what challenges you'll be faced with or how you'll overcome them. They just might prove to be something you can easily handle with your current abilities. And when the next challenge appears, the next opportunity to learn will present itself so that you can make the most of it. You don't have to know and do it all at once.

Guidelines

☼ **Think about what it is you really want.** What do you want Life to bring to you? Perhaps it's many things. Write them down on a piece of paper as a reminder and look at them often, preferably every day before going to sleep.

☼ **Be truthful to yourself.** If you want something that you are afraid to admit to others, that's understandable. But it is extremely important to admit it to yourself even if you find it is somehow not allowed. It may bring up unwanted emotions but they will pass, and a clear path will reveal itself.

☼ **Take action.** It is very important to plan, but it is just as important to act. By trying something, you will be pointed in the direction of your next step. Take opportunities, accept help, and see what's behind the corner.

☼ **This journey is about becoming.** For things in your life to change, you need to be willing to change some of your habits, beliefs, and other things to match the frequency of your wishes. If you stick to what you have been doing (and thinking about) so far, you'll be getting more of the same.

2.

MEETING CHANGE FACE TO FACE

"The secret of change is to focus all of your energy not on fighting the old, but on building the new."

Socrates

I haven't met a person to date that wasn't scared of or at least very nervous about change. Change is something that our mind perceives as potentially dangerous and we are majorly averted from it. We feel safe where we are, but staying in one place for long may result in boredom, which becomes more and more unbearable with time. Boredom might seem like a minuscule thing that you can shoo off like a fly whenever you want to, but it turns out that prolonged boredom can be a little bit more serious than it looks. It can easily turn into a deep state of avolition, depression, or even certain addictions. This is not to say that boredom is the underlying factor, but it can significantly attribute to all of the above.

As most of us already know, **change is the only constant in life**. There is nothing more certain that the fact that the situation you are currently in is going to change at some point in time. When we try to force something to stand still, we are literally creating a build-up of large amounts of energy. Because the nature of energy is to move, it will push against this blockage and inevitably evoke change, whether we want it or not. Learn to see change as an opportunity and turn it to our advantage. We can also embrace the feeling of uncertainty and fear accompanying it and learn to trust in our own abilities. Change is not the enemy. It is simply a means toward a different outcome. If you do things the same way over and over again, you can't expect your life to become better.

When you have no experience in trying something for the first time or going about it differently, it's similar to stepping onto an unlit path with only the flame of a burning candle to light the way. You have no idea whether you're stepping onto a slippery stone, into a thorny bush, or on soft moss or sand. It's dark and your imagination is running wild with all that might be lurking under your feet. Having a small flame to light the path is not enough to be able to step confidently. And that's scary for anyone. **The only path that is not scary is the one you have trodden over and over again**, the one you already know by heart. But if the path that you already know is not getting you to where you want to be, then taking a small indecisive step in another badly lit direction seems like a really good choice.

Apart from stepping into unknown territory, other people telling you how hard it's going to be is another thing that makes change scary. Let me tell you this: people who are trying to deter you from trying something new, are either too scared to make the leap themselves, or have already tried and have given up. They are secretly envious of anyone else who shows the courage to give it a go. They might not even know it consciously, but they go by the "if I can't do it, no one can" attitude. In fact, these are the people you would do better not to discuss your plans with or anything regarding them. Especially if you are scared and unsure of yourself. Stick to people who are at least one step ahead of you or those who believe in your abilities and never stop rooting for you, encouraging you to keep going.

How do you know the path you are taking is the right one for you? You never can be one hundred percent sure. Usually, it's something you've always wanted, something that has been at the back of your mind for a long time. Something you really, really want to try or can't imagine living without. **It is wise not to strive for success only, but for fulfillment especially.** The two are nowhere near similar. You can have great success and still be left with an emptiness inside, and you can have fulfillment in something seemingly small and meaningless, but it can give you so much joy you wouldn't change it for the world. Of course, the two combined are always possible, but not necessary. The most important thing is to have success in fulfilling your life's dream and purpose.

And what if you fail? You can always try again, move to a different place, change that job, leave that partner or sell whatever it is you have found not to be working for you. There is always an option to choose another path altogether as well. And no, you are never too old or too _____ to start over or try something you have never tried before. The worst thing that can happen is you end up with more experience and that is a treasure in itself. **It is not by making mistakes that you fail, but by not picking yourself up again and having another go.** As many times as it takes.

We often think embarking on something completely new will by some miracle get easy or at least easier. We sometimes imagine that when we are more prepared, less scared, when we build up our self-esteem or grow a pair, when the children grow up, when we have learned this and that, when we lose or gain weight, when we are less stressed, when we retire, we will be more ready to take the first step. Please remember that trying out new things, especially challenging things that you have never thought of trying before, is always scary and you will never be prepared enough to make the fear disappear. No matter who you are or how many pairs you may have managed to grow, stepping into the unknown is always accompanied by an uncomfortable amount of fear if not sometimes terror in the very beginning.

But there should inevitably be a sense of excitement somewhere in the background too, a sense of "I can hardly wait to get there". There should be a premonition that there might be something better for you somewhere other than where you are, and that taking steps in another direction just might get you to a better life eventually. It could turn out to be the best thing you have ever done for yourself, but you can never know until you try.

By trying out new things, learning from your mistakes, and getting to know your own strengths, you slowly start building trust in your own abilities. You begin trusting your instincts, building an inner library of good results, and having faith in yourself, to be able to get back on your feet again and again, should you happen to fall. This is what gives you courage and this is what gets you through the fear. The "I can do this" becomes stronger and stronger and a few slip-ups on the way seem to be minor or temporary hurdles. These hurdles become less and less important, and eventually, you take them as something that simply needs to be done. Perhaps not pleasant, but necessary. Similar to brushing your teeth before bed – it isn't fun, you just do it.

You begin to develop self-trust which is the most important tool you will ever have, by far. Self-trust develops slowly, one experience at a time, and you will start getting to know a part of you that you never imagined could exist. You will find you never knew you could be the person you have become, so courageous and daring. **You will get to see how your limitations were in fact only beliefs,** and have been of no service to the you that you were meant to be. I'm not saying everybody is capable of absolutely anything, but wouldn't it be great to find out how capable you actually are?

Any change is usually met with resistance. I would encourage you not to dwell upon the thing you are resisting for long. Not to list all of the things that could go wrong nor imagine a worst-case scenario. It is good to take a look at your weaknesses, at the tools you might need, but focusing more on what it is you want in life should be what you are investing most of your energy in. Your abilities may not be what you want them to be at the moment, but who's to say they can't grow? Ponder upon where you want to be, write about it, draw it, read about it, ... anything that will keep your mind turned forward. It may not be easy at first, but well worth the effort as this will make the path much smoother.

Guidelines

☼ **Change is bound to come in one way or another.** So why not design it to your advantage? Think of yourself as the driver of your life and observe how your situations gradually change when you choose to do things differently, react differently and try out something you have never tried before. Observe how everything is connected.

☼ **What would your life look like if there were no limitations?** Write it down. Examine how many of the limitations are in your mind and how many are outer circumstances. Can either be changed? How? What do you need to make this happen?

☼ **What are the limitations that could prevent you from succeeding?** In what way? Can they be changed? Can they be overcome? How? If not, why not? Examine which of the limitations are true and which are based on your fear or negative past experiences. What do you think your life will look like if you stay where you are? Do you want to stay there indefinitely? Why/why not?

☼ **What will the change you want to make bring you?** Will it enrich your life? In what way(s)? Why do you want whatever it is you want? Get to the core of your wishes so that you don't spend your time on trivia.

3.
FUELING THE FIRE

"If you are working on something that you really care about, you don't have to be pushed. The vision pulls you."

Steve Jobs

Whenever you make significant changes in your life, the most important thing that will keep you motivated enough to make it work is to **keep your vision alive as often as possible.** As well as visualizing it, talk about it, meditate on it, look at pictures related to it, watch videos, listen to others working on the same thing, and anything else you can think of to keep your mind engaged with it.

You reading this book is not a coincidence. The succession of events in your life has brought you to it and it is just another piece of the puzzle. Although you may already know some of the things portrayed here, there still might be something fresh that may evoke a new spark to get you to the next step. That's how life works for those who actively follow their dreams. An idea here, a suggestion there, one step back, three forward, and perhaps a period of being still to think things through. **One usually doesn't see further than the next step and it is a road unique to you.** No one can tell you how to do it step by step. You can't copy someone else's journey and expect exactly the same results. You are not that person. You have different things to learn, different skills to obtain, and different things to let go of. Each journey is one of a kind. Others can point you in the right direction, but it is you who needs to start taking action. Taking your own steps just might lead to treasures that will help you along the way.

Another way to keep you going is to **focus on the things that**

excite you. This will lead you in the right direction, even if it seems silly or irrelevant. Who's to say what your life is meant to look like? The excitement you feel when going towards a certain thing is the thing pointing towards your true path. It's being revealed milestone by milestone and what you feel when you think about it is significant. If you become afraid, try and look at what is beneath the fear. If it feels like enthusiasm or excitement, it is worth looking into. You never know where it might lead you to.

The number one priority of actualizing something you have always wanted is having a passion for it, a burning that stirs up your entire being. **The small steps you take toward it will fuel this fire and not let it go out.** The first step is just getting to know the territory, gathering data, and evaluating your options. **Research makes deciding what to do much easier.** Turning in the direction that you feel excited about will keep you on track. Whether or not you follow it is determined by how your mind interprets the task in front of you. Let's say you're longing to play the piano well, but you are not putting in the practice, because you're holding onto a belief that it is really difficult, or that you are perhaps not talented enough. And so you decide it is not worth your time, but the longing is still there, now turned into pain. Perhaps it would have become exciting if only you had sat at the piano and played just a little each day. By the end of the year, you could have become quite good at it.

There is a fire of excitement in all of us. When we are children it burns bright. It gives us the energy to keep discovering new things, making life literally magical. As we age, we forget to go where we feel excitement the most, and we are conformed to rules and regulations, becoming number with every passing year. So perhaps it is time to take a good look at your current life and start feeling, not just thinking or looking to others for answers. **Following the things you are excited about is what gives colour and meaning to life.** It doesn't have to be something big, but it does have to mean something special to you. It's your life and you have every right to actually live it the way you want to. Your task is to keep your inner fire going.

Guidelines

- ☼ **Visualize what it is that you want in your life as often as you can.** Cut out pictures, put them on your wall, write about it, imagine it as often as possible. Surround yourself with things that remind you of what it is you desire.

- ☼ **Research.** See what others are doing, look at what is available, read books, watch videos... Create an internal library of what the future you want looks like. This will help you make decisions and keep you pointed in the right direction.

- ☼ **Make your journey unique.** Use your imagination to plan it out and try out anything that sparks your interest and makes you feel excited about your goal.

4.
EMBRACING FEAR

"Thinking will not overcome fear but action will."

W. Clement Stone

Prolonged fear robs us of the ability to expand and live a joyous life. It plays a huge role in the destructive side of our society. It stirs up aggression and keeps people stuck in uncomfortable places. It makes us chronically worried, tense, anxious and can eventually lead to chronic illnesses. Fear brings stress into the body, making the adrenal glands work overtime, releasing large amounts of stress hormones. The adrenal glands are the ones that turn the autonomic nervous system on and off and when they are active, the body can't clean out its waste or regenerate cells. This creates acidity in the body, which leads to a number of physical and mental ailments. It also affects breathing, pooping, thinking, and sleeping.

If we want fear to subside eventually, it must be looked at. And looked at as objectively as possible. It is good to determine what it is that we are afraid of and what we expect to happen should this fear be realized. Feeding into it is not the goal, but looking if the outside circumstances are in fact dangerous, or if the fear is simply a product of our imagination and past traumas.

We are often afraid to keep going or sometimes to even begin because we expect the worst-case scenario. I always had a problem with procrastination, always waiting till the very last minute to finish a task. Being stressed out by the thought of actually doing something useful, I tried to avoid it until it could be avoided no longer. And all because of a profound fear of something going terribly wrong one way or the other. But it usually never did, apart from times when I was so fearful and stressed out by it, that I couldn't finish the task on time.

The mind tries to trick us into standing still, safely tucked in our reliable little corner. It has many different strategies to keep us as safe as possible. **What the mind perceives as safe, is what it is already familiar with.** Anything different from the data it possesses is labeled with a large question mark. Keeping you safe is the mind's number one priority. It actively looks for danger, because most of us have been brought up to do so. Look out, be careful, don't climb that tree or you'll fall, watch your step, and so on. If you hear these things often enough, your mind learns that being focused on potential danger is more important than having a good time. The more we focus on danger, the more of it we see, and in some extremes, we start imagining it's there even when it's not.

Fear stems for the most part from negative thoughts that have nothing to do with our actual situation. We watch the news and imagine the same happening to us. We replay thoughts from a traumatic event to which the body reacts as if it is actually happening right now. And so we miss what is really going on around us, unable to stay focused and relaxed. Fear can also be born out of a lack of information (or out of missinformation). We need to know enough about a subject to understand what is actually going on, what to expect, how to react, etc. The less we know, the more foreign it is, and the greater the possibility of us being afraid of it.

To find out if what you are about to do is in fact dangerous in any way, you need to take a closer look. Get informed about it, and that will most probably reduce your fear considerably. But know that risks are always accompanied by a certain amount of fear. People who do risky things often are not fearless, they just know that fear is short-lived, not permanent. They are used to having it as a companion when they embark on something unknown. **The beginning frightening stages of fear will always subside by getting more experience.** When you have repeated something often enough for it to become known, the fear will be minimal, none at all, or you will have gotten so used to it, that you won't even pay attention to it anymore. You might only accept your body's reaction to it, just like you would sitting on an airplane that is taking off. You probably don't enjoy it, but it passes. And once you're above the clouds, you simply enjoy the view.

Fear of change is crippling for most people because they imagine the worst-case scenario being played out in their future. Sometimes by imagining a better future, we are trying to envision our goal far, far away from where we are. It is normal not to be able to see that far ahead, especially if you are at the beginning of your journey. And so a picture of what it looks like is left entirely to your imagination. Being afraid of it or not then depends greatly on what you are imagining it to be.

Imagine your starting point being somewhere in a valley and your goal being somewhere behind the mountain. There is absolutely no way you could see the road from the beginning to the end. Just do the best you can and keep going. If you are having difficulty envisioning a positive outcome, start small. Try to imagine the next couple of steps. Try to paint a picture of what it would look like to take the first step, letting the outcome be in your favour. By doing this, your steps won't seem daunting anymore, because you will have already made them in your imagination. You needn't have it all planned out, as life is unpredictable sometimes. **You just need to have an approximate picture of what it is you want and hold it close to your heart and mind.** The rest will unfold as you go.

But let me stress that it is important you try and see the life you truly want, not the life that "could, possibly, if things happen to work out, be a little better than the one you're living now". Aim high. There is almost nothing that can hinder your success other than yourself and the way you react to certain circumstances. Here lies your power and the things that you can control are your thoughts, your reactions, and your actions.

When you find fear rearing up its ugly head, remember that this is a memory, a program still stuck somewhere between your brain cells. When you acquire enough information and get some experience, it gets more manageable until managing it is something you can do with your eyes closed. You gain trust in yourself, which needs to be built like you would build trust with another person. **You learn to trust yourself by taking care of your own needs.** It's like becoming your own parent. Granted, it's not always easy, but if you choose to expect a good outcome and envision it often, it can start to become fun and exciting. Then fewer and fewer things become an issue and fear is something that comes and goes without getting stuck in your body and mind.

The fear of making mistakes is very often the very thing that stops people in their tracks. But mistakes are simply landmarks. It's the way the Universe (or Life or God or whatever it is you choose to call it) corrects our way. **It is you who chooses the goal and it is the Universe who decides how, where and when** it will come. Making a mistake is simply missing the mark. Try again, try it differently again and again, until you get it right or get it done.

Mistakes do not define who you are. No one has been born with knowledge, only instinct. You need to learn certain things if you want to be good or even average at something. By the way, being average at something is no less than being good or excellent at it. Depending on your goal and wishes, average results can be enough for you to be able to live the way you want to. You don't have to be the best. You get to be the best if you strive to never stop learning, but if being the best is your goal, then I suggest you look at what it is you imagine you'll be getting with this title. You most certainly do not have to be best at anything to have a fulfilled and joyous life. More often than not, average is all it takes.

It is a controversial idea in our society, but the fact of life is that **the more mistakes you are prepared to make, the faster you will learn and the quicker you will get results.** Being willing to make mistakes and letting them go by moving forward, having a mindset of certainty that you will eventually get there, taking small steps each and every day, and taking care of your body-mind are the four main pillars of building a dream life. The mistakes you are making are merely pebbles of wisdom you are picking up along the way. **"Keep going" is a good mantra to have.**

Always remember: this too shall pass. Whatever it is you are struggling with on your journey forward, it will pass even quicker, if you take action to wiggle out of the predicament. Expect good things to happen even though it might seem they are not turning out the way you hoped they would. Remember that the only way you can fail is by quitting. If you decide not to quit, you will inevitably come to a solution in time, as there is always chaos within change, and eventually, things fall always into place one way or the other. Just keep going, adjusting your course as you go.

Guidelines

- ☼ **Look at your situation closely.** Write down exactly what it is you're afraid of. Anything that is happening now or that might happen to you in the future. Be as specific as you wish.

- ☼ **Feel the fear when it comes up.** Don't try to avoid it, or it will keep you stuck in place. Just feel it in your body, and observe what that's like. Stay with the feeling and let it move wherever it wants to. Let it express itself in whichever form it wants (that is safe for you and others). This can be through crying, shaking, making sounds, etc. Choose a safe environment and ask someone you trust to do this with you, if you feel you need support. You can always go to a good therapist who can lead you through it.

☼ **Use your imagination to play out a positive scenario.** Whenever you are afraid something bad will happen, try imagining the exact opposite, and imagine it in your mind as vividly as possible. Choose the most positive scenario you can find. This might not be simple at first, but repeat it as many times as you can, until you have no problem imagining a positive outcome.

☼ **Always strive to get things done, not to get them done perfectly.** Make this your goal. Finish what you start. What it looks like is not important. As you get more comfortable with this new change you have made, when you obtain more courage, self-confidence, and self-discipline, then you can focus on the quality, not before.

☼ **Keep going when you fail.** It is normal to fail sometimes, try not to take it as an indication of how capable you are. Your ability to pick yourself up and keep going is what you need to work on and it is the only thing that really matters.

5.
BEING WILLING TO LEARN

"There is no failure. You win or you learn. Either one is okay."

Gary Keller

We often imagine life as being a succession of events and actions but actually, nothing in life is linear and no path in nature is a straight line. **Everything is intertwined very tightly, making it literally a web of energy.** If the web is changed at one end, the whole web gets restructured. Learning is the main ingredient with which you can change this web to your advantage. Good things will come to you if you just do your thing and stop focusing on the outcome. It really speeds things up if you learn to enjoy the process.

Learning new things will broaden your horizon and will give you a feeling of security. Like a larder filled with food, money in the bank, or a woodshed full of firewood do. Knowledge gives you power because with it comes self-confidence and self-reliance. You learn to trust in your ability to get the tools you need and to learn how to use them. So you stop relying only on others and start taking things into your own hands.

It is very important to learn from your own mistakes, much more than from other people's. By making mistakes, you really integrate the knowledge and never forget it. **Learning without experience is not learning,** it's theory. Learning is the most valuable thing in life and unless you are willing to learn by taking your own steps, you can't expand and your life can't evolve. If you simply repeat what others have done before you and rely only on their knowledge, you can't really get to where you want to go.

When I was thinking of how to go about writing this book, I realized that every success in my life is in fact based on my previous actions and my previous knowledge, no matter how meaningless it might have seemed at the time. If one thing hadn't happened this way, the other might not have come out that way, and so on. You might have noticed the same if you have been paying attention. **Everything you have learned up till now has come in handy and those things that haven't yet, are bound to.** If in fact, you have been paying attention and have been learning from your mistakes.

We often choose not to learn anything when faced with difficult situations, but when we do, we see the difficulty as having been just a messenger of a life lesson that helped us grow. If we are not paying attention though, it will most definitely repeat itself in one form or another. By trying to do something different from what you did the previous time, you can achieve different results. **Doing more of the same will get you more of the same.** When you pay attention and learn, the lesson is finished and you become richer for it, making your life a little easier every time.

Learning is a never-ending process and has absolutely nothing to do with the school system, or with ideas, that the advertising industry together with the media has been trying to fill our brains with. **Learning has to do with information, action, and experience.** With adequate information, we can take action and get more experience. This is true learning. Schools usually promote memorizing, not learning. As obvious as it may sound, we forget that experience is possible only by taking action, not by reading about it or by merely observing it. It is completely different when you yourself go through something and far more enriching. Watching someone else get and become what you want for yourself, can help with motivation, but you're not going to get there unless you take action yourself.

The combination of information, action, and experience brings faith. Faith in yourself and your abilities, faith in others, faith in a higher power, and faith in whatever else you happen to need faith for. By actively participating in your own life, you begin to see that **you are a significant part of the great force that governs your fate.** You in fact are the captain of the ship that represents your life. And as well you know, the captain knows little about managing the engine room that keeps the ship going. She/he doesn't know everything about the bolts and screws, and she/he most definitely can't command the wind and the sea. The captain makes decisions based on her/his experience, knowledge, and intuition. The same goes for you. If something goes wrong, it is your responsibility to come away with more experience, and try better next time. And the most important thing is to learn from your mistakes and get wise(r).

The way to learn from failure is to reflect with hindsight, on what the situation was trying to teach you. When your emotions have calmed down of course. Do you need to learn a new skill, could your communication be clearer, is your perception or belief false or outdated, do you perhaps need to gather more information? Life is about growing, becoming stronger, more agile, wiser, and living in a better and more fulfilled way. If you choose not to learn from the mistakes you make, you are bound to eventually get stuck, and with that comes misery.

Another thing you would benefit greatly from is **investing money and time in broadening your knowledge.** Think of books, seminars, lectures, and other forms of professional guidance as an investment in your future. This is your treasure chest that you can take from for the rest of your life. If you feel a certain thing will give you the information you are lacking, it is never time or money wasted, but invested and can help you a great deal in the long run. You can figure it out on your own too, but it will take much longer than it would if you paid for that course or bought that book. Of course with the technology we have nowadays, you get so much information for free too, so be sure to take advantage of that.

Everything on this planet grows while it is alive and it is in your nature to do the same. It is up to you to find out which way you want to go and where it is you want to end up. Your task is to imagine, plan, reflect and take small frequent steps, even when you have no idea if they are going to work. The rest will be taken care of on its own. By doing your part, you set the whole energetic machinery in motion, and the laws of this Universe will do the rest. All you have to do is find out if this is what you truly want and take the journey. **Keep at it and all will come to fruition with time.** Never stop learning.

Guidelines

☼ **Allow yourself to make mistakes and learn from them.** When you make a mistake, look at what it is you need to adjust next time. Look at what tools you are missing and which knowledge you need to acquire. Feel the disappointment if it's there, but know that this has only been a learning curve and that the next opportunity will come if you keep going. You'll get there eventually and you won't be starting from scratch but from experience.

☼ **Invest time and money into your treasure chest of knowledge.** Go to seminars, get books, take classes, watch free videos, etc. Learn from people who have similar interests or that are a couple of steps ahead. Look for new ways to get to where it is you want to be. Educate yourself on what it looks like and never stop learning.

☼ **Study, plan, and then take action.** This is the only way to really harness the true power of knowledge. Through action, you will make mistakes and learn from them, which is the fastest route to success. This way, you will also gain trust in your abilities.

6.
REDIRECTING YOUR FOCUS

*"You get what you focus on.
So focus on what you want."*

Steve Mehr

What you focus on predominantly, becomes a magnet that starts automatically pulling you in its direction. The longer your focus is turned in a certain direction, the stronger the magnet becomes. Anything you do will be influenced by it. And if you are not really satisfied with where you're being pulled towards, it might be hard at first to change the direction of that magnetic pull. So if your focus is on the problem instead of on finding the solution, the bigger the problem will seem and the less possible it will be to resolve it. Many get pulled into worst-case scenarios automatically and keep reliving their frustration over and over. It is impossible to get somewhere new if you don't learn to focus on where you want to be going instead of where you are now or where you have been in the past.

I feel obligated to stress the importance of redirecting your thoughts. Constantly thinking about things that you wish would go away, brings chronic stress into your everyday life, not to mention the damage it does to your physical and mental health. No one can function well, never mind having a positive attitude about their future, by being under chronic stress. Thinking about what went wrong in the past, what is going wrong now, or what could go wrong in the future, brings you into a state that kills both creativity and motivation. I hear you, it's hard. Especially if you're in a really difficult predicament and you haven't been able to see a way out for ages. You will need to practice.

There is no way redirecting your thoughts can be achieved overnight, especially if you have been on autopilot for the majority of your life, letting any thoughts come and go as they please. I know many people who believe thoughts are just something that happens to them and they can't do anything about which ones decide to come. They believe we have thoughts. But in reality, we produce thoughts. **Thoughts are your interpretation of the situation you find yourself in** and may be quite different from the way things actually are.

Have you heard of the saying "change the way you look at things and the things you look at change"? Well, **looking at things differently is taking control of your own thoughts**, steering them to help you get to where you are heading, eventually changing your surroundings. Not by putting energy into making them go away, but by changing your perspective and seeing them differently. With this, you will see which actions to take more clearly. Practicing thinking of what it is you want instead of what is troubling you, is a tool that changes a whole series of events.

Why is redirecting our thoughts so difficult? We can do it for a couple of seconds, but people who have a predominantly negative outlook on life, find it impossible to sustain. This is because **negative thoughts are extremely addictive.** You can get addicted to the amount of stress hormone released in your blood and although it doesn't feel good, you can't seem to stop, searching for something negative to chew on all the time. Whether it be bad news, some scandal, something horrible someone said, or some tragedy that occurred.

We all know people who seem to have a direct landline to all of the unhappiness in this world. They know only of the bad as if the good didn't exist. These people feel comfortable in this negative state, and yet they are very unhappy. Being relaxed is something completely out of the ordinary for them. When we want to change for the better, our mindset needs to be altered in such a way that it starts **looking for opportunities rather than fishing for the next catastrophe.**

Imagine your mind as being your child. Someone who is often scared, is always on the lookout for danger and pain, figuring out ways to avoid them before they even emerge. It is trying to do everything in its power to keep you where you are because it knows how to control the outcome from there. It believes the world is the way you were taught it was when you were very little. And yet **the world is an energetic web loaded with different opportunities and different ways to be.** That is a fact. There are endless ways to be and endless ways to live. How many of these ways you see, is all up to the flexibility of your imagination. If it's rusty, you need to get it working again.

You can observe children that are allowed to use their

imagination, they are never still or bored, and find endless opportunities for adventure without being afraid of what they might run into. Even if there is a monster lurking in the shadowy corner, they soon invent an invisible device, word, or some other tactic, that gets rid of it. And they become invincible if only they are allowed to explore new possibilities.

The power of imagination and visualization is underrated by most people. When you learn to imagine your future and visualize it to the extent of feeling like you're already there, things start to become fluent and events and opportunities that take you there emerge. Your mind gets new assignments and stops going over what has happened in the past. Visualizing a positive outcome also reduces stress in the body and calms the nervous system.

Your focus is like a steering wheel. You can turn it in whichever direction you want, you just need to be willing to take it into your own hands. And to do this, you first need to be aware that you actually can. We often think of life as something that is happening to us, but we can actually learn to navigate well in its waters. As the song goes: "**I can't control the wind, but I can adjust the sail**". The whole point is learning to sail through life, and then there is no dilemma about whether or not you can reach your destination. Focusing your mind on where you want to go is the first step. And then adjust the course as you go.

It is not only the visualization that is important. **It is action that is the wind against your sails.** A combination of the right focus and action is what will keep the boat of your life going. So focus first, then take action. And remember, you don't need to do it perfectly as the point of being on this journey of life is to learn, change and be playful, not perfect.

Guidelines

☼ **Learn to redirect your thoughts.** It sounds simple, and I know it's not. You need to practice. When you catch a thought that doesn't serve you and it keeps repeating itself, try turning to your imagination and either think of a different course things are going to take or imagine something different altogether (an object, place, etc). Some people have a »happy place« they go to in their mind, some sort of a neutral zone they can continue from. Find what works for you and practice. It will get easier.

☼ **When you find yourself in a whirlwind of negative thoughts, look for the feeling underneath.** Sometimes, our mind is trying to prevent us from feeling certain uncomfortable emotions and it starts looking for ways to do so. And so the »monkey mind« is born. When you find your mind being overwhelmed by anxious thoughts, stop, and feel your body. Stay with it until an emotion surfaces, and then let it out.

☼ **Imagine where you want to be, as often as you can.** Your imagination has so much power and the more times you imagine yourself in situations you want to be in, the more accustomed your mind will become with them, and the more it will start to let go.

☼ **Focus on what you want, not what you don't want.** What you focus on grows and when you find yourself in a difficult situation, use your energy to find answers and visualize what the solution might look like. This will help you immensely to get back on track. It will also help you stay motivated and save to do what needs to be done.

7. WORKING FOR THE GOOD OF ALL

"The good man is friend to all living things"

Mahatma Gandhi

Wanting good for yourself and all other beings on this planet will bring you to true fulfillment the fastest. Neglecting either will always be a hindrance to you in the long run. We all know of selfish people who only want good for themselves and not many people are eager for them to get far. On the other hand, people often applaud those who want good things for others, and yet neglect their own needs. These people usually end up resentful, depressed, and lonely, even if only on the inside, and they don't enjoy life much.

A healthy way to take care of others is to **fulfill your needs and wishes so profusely that your joy and love of life spreads to them on its own.** This happens naturally and without effort. When you fulfill your needs and enrich your life by feeding your soul and taking care of your own happiness, you automatically become a good person and good deeds and kindness come naturally to you without effort.

Gaining something for yourself at the cost of other beings, won't lead you to a calm and enriched life. It may make you wealthy, it may even make you popular, but it will not bring you peace, love, or freedom. It is a known fact that rich people have reported that the most important things in their life didn't come with wealth or fame. Having enough money to buy anything you desire is splendid, but what good is that if you're just as unhappy with it as you were without it? So make sure you think well and hard about what it is that you really want. Make sure this can truly be bought before you go on a quest of striving for wealth.

The more you work towards a better world for all beings, the happier and more peaceful your life will become. Doing good for others extends into all of the natural world, not just people. We are born from Nature and are enmeshed with it as a seed is enmeshed with fruit, as a wave is part of the ocean, as warmth is part of the sun, as a branch is part of a tree. We are all part of an energetic web that is intertwined with absolutely everything, stretching far into the Universe. Our little lives in our little boxes often disable us from seeing the big picture. But those who can open their eyes to it get access to the neverending abundance of this stream of life's energy and with it everything it can provide.

Guidelines

☼ **Look at the big picture.** Whatever it is you are desiring, always check if it is something that will benefit you, other people, and Nature as well, or check that it is at least not harmful to any of the three.

☼ **Focus on fulfilling your own needs first:** the need to be seen and heard; the need to work, play, and rest; the need for shelter, food; the need for connection and love; the need for boundaries; the need for growth and safety. Focus on getting the assistance you need if you can't do it alone. But remember: your happiness is your own responsibility.

8.
LISTENING TO YOUR INNER GUIDANCE

"All I need to know at any given moment is revealed to me. My intuition is always by my side"

Louise Hay

Every person has their own path, as our wishes vary. When you learn to navigate well, this path is smooth and the winds usually blow in your favour. Learning to navigate takes time, training, and refocusing every time you wander off your path. Steering your life in the direction you would like it to go takes getting to know your self and your body. **Your inner navigational system is predominantly made up of your emotions and your instincts.** They are your guides. Whatever feels good (in a calm way), is usually the right way to go, and whatever doesn't, is not - at the moment anyway. Each one of us possesses an inner compass that provides us with the ability to choose the right course, but the trick is to learn to pay attention to it. Most of us are unaware that our wishes may stem from our old beliefs that have been passed on to us from our parents and friends, and are in fact not true to who we are. But when we learn to listen to what we truly feel, and what our inner navigation system is telling us, everything runs smoothly most of the time.

Instincts are built into our body's electric system and represent what we call our "gut feeling". It is never wrong but is harder to acknowledge because most of us have been taught in our early years to ignore it, and pay more attention to doing what is acceptable to others. All in all, when you are faced with the question of what to do next, whether to trust someone or not, to take certain risks, etc, **your gut feeling is always the right one to listen to.** When you experience fear, but your gut feeling is telling you to go for it anyway (or perhaps not), it is always right. Your mind, on the other hand, does not have this ability. Your task is to train yourself to listen to your instincts, not your mind, which can be quite a daunting task in the beginning, as it can be hard to differentiate between the two. But through practice, anyone can learn to recognize one from the other.

Intuition is your inbuilt radar that is directly connected to Nature and the Cosmos. It is your power line to the fastest way of getting where it is you want to go. Your instincts are not something you acquire, but are primal and have more to do with the body's intelligence than the mind's. Intuition is connected to your energy field and is in tune with your well-being. It is a guide to keep you safe and well. Ignoring it completely brings your body/mind into disarray and turns your path into a labyrinth.

Another thing that shouldn't be suppressed or ignored are your wishes. **The role of every wish is to bring you to a place of growth.** When the wish is realized and the lessons learned, then the wish doesn't have a hold on you anymore. For example, if you desire money but are still not satisfied even though you have obtained the desired amount, you have not yet learned the lesson you were supposed to. When enough roads have been taken, enough mistakes made, enough lessons learned, enough wisdom gained, you feel content with your life, and you learn to enjoy to simply be. Whenever you feel the need to move – either by wanting something or by going somewhere – there is something for you there and it is good to take a look at what that is. Our instincts will tell us if it is something that benefits us, or if it needs to be avoided. Listening to them can prevent you from wasting your time and from getting hurt.

Guidelines

☼ **Pay special attention o your body.** It will always be a good indicator if you are making the right decision. Don't obsess over making the right choice though, as you need practice to get back in touch with your intuition. Just pay attention to how your body feels and pay also attention to your dreams. Again, please don't try to decipher their meaning, just plug into the feeling they leave you with. You'll soon learn the language of the body/mind if you give it some time and attention.

☼ **Learn to differentiate your thoughts from your feelings.** Emotions are sometimes derived from thought, especially fear and anger. If you take the time to observe which is which once in a while, you'll soon feel the difference. Your intuition is more of a feeling in the body that is instant. It's more of a »yes« or »no« feeling, not so much the debris of emotions around that.

☼ **Make decisions in a state of calmness.** When you research, think things through, and check-in with your body, you'll usually know what to do, even if it feels scary. Just dip your toe in and see what it looks like. You'll do the right thing more times than not. And if not, you'll learn a lot if willing.

9.
TRYING UNTIL YOU SUCCEED

"Every accomplishment starts with the decision to try."

John F. Kennedy

Setting a goal means it may not be met in the timeframe you had in mind. And that is not an indicator that you have failed, but can be because of a myriad of things: skills yet to be acquired, things to be learned, others to be let go of, and perhaps plans to be changed. **It is only when you stop trying that you can justifiably say that you have failed.** But when you keep going, you are on your way to getting what it is that you want. Just as it is darkest just before dawn, so too is the chaos greatest just before change occurs.

A lot of people, unfortunately, quit right before the results start coming in or an opportunity reveals itself. So be aware of that when the going gets tough, which it may sometimes. Be also aware that although things may sometimes take longer to achieve than you thought, the opposite is also true. Sometimes something that might have seemed difficult may prove to be easily playful and may take no time at all to accomplish. The important thing is to keep an open mind and believe in your abilities even when it feels like you couldn't possibly do the thing that needs to be done.

We are often poisoned by the "I can't" mentality. How do you know you can't? Because you have tried once and didn't succeed? All right, you tried three times? The number of times you need to try to succeed is as many as it takes. This doesn't mean rigidly sticking to just one way of doing something until you are depleted of all your energy, but trying different things in different ways, changing what needs to be changed, and sometimes, even asking for help. That is the recipe. Add something new, take something away, call someone and ask for advice, take a course, change your list of goals, turn off the phone, wifi, TV, meditate, go and see a financial adviser, exercise regularly, take a risk, partner up with someone, rest, join that dating site, research, take notes, see what else is out there, look for solutions and ways out of predicaments, eat healthy food, get enough sleep, learn at every opportunity, breathe... Anything you can think of that supports your goal. **It's the next piece of the puzzle that helps you grow** and helps make you the person that will vibrate on the same level as your dream life.

It is the small things you do every day that make a difference, not the big things you do every so often. Anything and everything you do for the better is valuable, nothing that you try that could contribute to meeting your goals is useless or trivial, even if it might seem so. And if you fail? Try again, do it better or do it differently. Try whatever intrigues you that someone else is doing, and see if it works for you, read books, watch videos, have deep conversations, and ask people who are one or more steps ahead. **Get answers, but more importantly, ask the right questions.** And always take the next step, until you are happy to be where you are.

There will be days when you will most definitely feel like giving up. Just like building your physical muscles takes time and is sometimes uncomfortable, so does the building of a more capable and joyful you. You need to train and build skills to become that person. It's not that you're not it and others are, you simply haven't taken the necessary steps they have. That means working on your procrastination, on your mindset, and learning how to calm the mind as well as obtaining certain skills needed for your particular goal.

Sometimes you will want to give up just because you can't be bothered anymore, or feel it's not worth the effort. And sometimes there will be a very good reason why this might seem like a good idea. It's okay to stop on those days, maybe it's just rest that you need. **You are allowed to give yourself a break, just make sure this break is not permanent.** Get back up when you can, and continue from where you left off. Start by taking small steps again and that will get the momentum going soon enough.

Sometimes doing just five minutes of what you should be doing is all that you can do. And that's always better than nothing. The danger of doing nothing for longer than necessary, is that you get used to it and it slowly starts nagging on your psyche, dragging you into uncomfortable states you need even more time and energy to get out of. We people are prone to inertia and everyone struggles with it unless you happen to be a workaholic, which is another problem altogether.

Sticking to something with the focus on getting it right eventually, will bring you knowledge and additional insights, together with new tools and experiences. It will make you stronger and more self-reliant. You find out what you are capable of, which is usually far more than you initially thought. My rule of thumb is to try something at least ten times before I start thinking of giving up. By the time I get to ten, the task is usually accomplished.

A really important part of not giving up is **learning to rest, not to quit if you feel overwhelmed and tired.** Take a break, reevaluate your situation, empty your mind and regroup. Taking good care of yourself and meeting your needs is an essential part of this. It is no use trying to get through a wall, and there just might be a door right next to you that you can't see. Sometimes all it takes is to take a step back and look at things from a different perspective.

Make trying repeatedly your norm. Life gets much easier if you do. Perhaps not in the beginning, but if you make a rule of getting over the preliminary fear and actively pushing through your insecurities every time, the rest becomes easier, and your motivation increases as you achieve small victories along the way. Just as getting to the top of the ladder takes many steps, so does getting to your goal.

Guidelines

☼ **Make it a habit to keep getting back up.** When you fail (and you will), dwell on the lesson you have been presented with. Not succeeding is not failing, it is just practice. Do your best and when you know more, do better.

☼ **If you do not succeed in doing something in a certain way, try doing it differently.** You can't get the same results if you keep trying to reach a goal from the same angle. Look for different approaches and consult with other people who have succeeded in doing the same. Try to build up the courage to reach out to someone you don't know.

☼ **Anything you do to make the smallest change counts.** Whether it be getting up earlier, exercising more, redirecting your thoughts, or taking the time to read a chapter of a book. Just keep going.

☼ **Do not expect instant gratification,** but do expect a favourable outcome eventually, just keep going. If you look, you will find. And if you get an idea for something better, more in tune with who you are, try that instead.

10.
GETTING TO KNOW YOUR MIND

"All problems are illusions of the mind"

Eckhart Tolle

It is often the case that our mind is trying to keep us stuck where we are because **it is designed to keep us safe**. Unfortunately, this means it will try to keep us there indefinitely unless we train it differently. The mind is just a structure of thought patterns that we have accumulated during our lifetime. To begin with, it is a pattern of borrowed ideas, beliefs, and rules, and our own interpretations of them. Until we consciously make the effort to change.

Let's take money as an example. If as children we have been told repeatedly that money is difficult to come by and requires great effort, it will have a profound effect on how stressed we are when making it. We might feel tired before even starting to earn some, our body being used to working very hard for it. Or we might perhaps have a difficult time accepting it when it is given to us because we don't feel worthy, and if we do accept it, will do our best to subconsciously get rid of it as soon as possible. No wonder it is impossible to enjoy money and the advantages it can bring, with a mindset like that. But if we have learned as children that money can be made easily through different means, then we can hardly wait to try out a new venture, not thinking about the money much, but enjoying and focusing on the process of making it.

If you have a mindset that money is something precious that is hard to come by and that you are lucky to have any at all, it will be hard to let go of it to – let's say – make a bigger profit, because you think of it as a treasure to be kept somewhere safe and hidden. On the other hand, if we view money as a means to help us get to where we want to be, we will regard it as a tool, which can easily be replaced, as tools tend to be. **If our mind is programmed to believe something is difficult, dangerous, or unpleasant, even if it may not be, we will have an adversity to it.** The same goes for relationships, new skills, taking risks, and other important things in life we would do well to try out and get better at.

Another thing regarding the mind that's worth paying attention to is overthinking and especially worrying. If you're like I used to be, you probably remind yourself of the things you should worry about the minute you wake up, which makes you want to stay in bed and do nothing. On the days that I didn't have to go to work, I used to spend hours wasting beautiful mornings, replaying negative things that had happened or could happen. Until I finally made one of the best decisions of my life, to start training my mind to work with, not against me, by redirecting my thoughts deliberately. It takes practice and it's not easy in the beginning, I won't lie. Because negative thinking needs to be treated like any other addiction. Worrying can be never-ending and it might seem like things are happening to you and that the thoughts you are thinking are an automatic reflection of your reality. But more often than not, this is not the case.

Of course, there are occasions when worry is an adequate response. But most of the time, it changes absolutely nothing except for making the body chronically stressed after a while, creating sickness as a consequence. Worry usually has to do with the interpretation of things that are happening. This interpretation is directly linked to our beliefs, and **beliefs are just thoughts being repeated over and over again.** It is possible to stop this stream of negative thinking and worrying, but it takes practice. The more you redirect your thoughts, the more you develop. You develop faith in a positive outcome and this starts being reflected in your everyday life. You also get to have more time in your day, freeing yourself from worry and angst, and you get to do more of the things that bring you closer to a life you actually want to be living.

The mind is directly connected to the body. The two are one and the same organism and thus function as a whole. They can in no way be separated. We usually address them separately, because ... well, it's a common way to look at them I guess. We can see one, but can't see the other. We can touch one, but not the other, and so on. The fact that the mind and body are different sides of the same coin, can help us understand that they will directly react to how the other is feeling.

The mind is a powerful computer but is still just a tool. When we let it take over, things start getting complicated. By taking control of your mind and what you are predominantly thinking of, you get the ability to change every single part of your life if you learn to use the mind to your advantage. **Literally change your mind, and your circumstances will slowly but surely start changing.** Just have faith in a positive outcome and it will happen.

Being like a computer, you can literally reprogramme the mind. Primarily, it is supposed to be a tool for survival and getting your needs met, but **when the need to survive surpasses the need to grow and expand, the mind starts taking the lead.** You can regain control by firstly being aware of what it is you think about often. Is it negative or positive? Are your thoughts fueled by fear or by faith in a positive outcome, regardless of the current circumstances? You can train your mind to be calmer and quieter. You don't want to shut it off completely because you need it to navigate. You need it to think and evaluate whatever obstacles you might encounter.

But calming it down will give you back your energy, having removed the unnecessary inner chatter. At least much of it anyway. You can quieten your mind through regular meditation or active relaxation, regular non-aggressive exercise, deep breathing, spending time in nature, and similar activities. But most of all, you can calm the mind by thinking about what it is that you want as often as possible and how to get to it. Catching that destructive thought and redirecting it to something productive, will in time restructure and reprogramme your mind. Perhaps not completely, but to a satisfying extent.

As your mind is also your inner voice, **it is important you talk to yourself as you would talk to someone you love and actually like.** Even if you're struggling with that, just try and adapt a friendly inner tone that would resemble the way you would like other people to talk to you. It should be kind and uplifting. The way you talk to yourself will reflect in your actions and in the amount of motivation you have, to be able to take care of your needs.

Guidelines

☼ **Do your best to make friends with your mind.** Imagine it is a small child and that it needs constant reassurance. Talk to it kindly and thank it for all its help when it wants to take control. It needs to be told that everything is all right and that it can let go. Let it know that you are capable of handling things and that there is no need to worry.

☼ **Establish an attitude of gratitude.** This will give you a feeling of safety and abundance. End your day with at least three things you are grateful for. On difficult days, even more.

☼ **Redirect your thoughts.** With this, you let the mind know that it is no longer in charge. It may rebel at first but by consistent redirection, it will soon get it. And when it does, it will start leaning in the direction you want to go and start working with you.

☼ **Use different tools that quieten the mind.** You don't want to shut it down, but only to relax the nervous system. This can be done with things like meditation, daily walks, etc.

11.
GETTING OFF AUTOPILOT MODE

"You either control your mind or it controls you."

Napoleon Hill

Frequently repeated thoughts become a pattern, which eventually becomes a habit. And once you're in a habitual pattern, you are not even paying attention to what you're doing anymore. Once you start changing your habits, you start being more alert and your days get much more interesting. Your life starts getting a different meaning that is more suited to who you are now. By changing your habits, you change the programming that might not be serving you, keeping you stuck in the past.

Small habits that we repeat every day are the ones that have the biggest impact on our future. They determine whether we'll stay on the same old path, getting the same old outcome, or not. Somewhere in our life, most of us have unfortunately lost the ability to be amazed by what life has to offer and so we stop looking at what else is possible. As children, we see the world as a magical place, filled with wonder, excitement, and opportunity. As we grow, we don't observe our surroundings directly through our own senses as much, but start focusing more on what is being pointed out to us by someone else. Be it someone on television, our parents, relatives, or our peers, and with time, we take this to be our predominant focus of attention. What is repeatedly pointed out to us, becomes what is "real", even though we may feel there might be something missing or not quite right. In our childhood, wanting to be accepted, loved, and nurtured is far more important than what is true to us.

And so we literally borrow a way to be, a way to see the world as well as ourselves and others, unwillingly ignoring what we are actually feeling, thinking, or seeing. We also subconsciously train our body to ignore its natural navigational system. Our reprogrammed mind starts dictating our life. In short, we start living on autopilot. The sad thing is, that many people stay on autopilot even when they grow up unless they are willing to change their programming.

What we read, listen to, watch and talk about is literally what our thoughts are going to consist of. So it is a good idea to choose these things wisely. Until I started paying attention, I had never noticed how much those things impacted my mood, my day, my decisions, and my whole life. I had never noticed before, how lyrics to songs impacted me, for example. The impact is not sudden and direct but seeps into your subconscious, each time you hear a certain lyric being repeated. Nowadays, I choose the songs I listen to carefully, and the things I watch and read too, as I know the words and pictures will eventually become engraved into my very being, especially if repeated often. If you are on a path to change your life for the better, if you want your days to be lighter and more uplifting, your visual and audio library should reflect that.

Did you know that watching the news releases a vast amount of stress hormones that significantly contribute to lowering your immune system? Bad news are the ones that sell and TV stations are on a hunt for the most shocking news out there to get the highest viewing rates. This makes the viewer think there is danger at every corner. Just observe how your body gets tense when you're watching a catastrophe being played out on the screen.

What you talk and think about often, will also most certainly affect your mood and train your mind on what to focus on. If you are complaining or gossiping a lot, if you frequently like to think and talk about all of the terrible things that happened in the past, you will gradually no longer be able to see goodness and kindness around you and as a consequence will start seeing the world as a negative and dangerous place where nothing pleasant ever happens and catastrophe lies behind every corner. This is not how the world is at all.

Now there is a difference between complaining and telling someone your troubles with the purpose of resolving an issue, getting help or advice. But continually complaining and not being willing to change anything, is extremely draining on the person listening. By focusing predominantly on negative things, you start thinking you're attracting them, that you have been born unlucky or are perhaps cursed even. If you think only bad things are going to happen to you, you'll start accepting them as fate and will stop saying no to them. People who expect good things from life say no to negative ones and try to change their situation for the better as soon as possible. They are always searching for a solution, a resolution, and a more favourable alternative because they know it's out there.

All of the above is not to say we should ignore the negative things around us. Not at all. The idea is to start training your mind to be alive and agile again to see **there is always an exchange of energy and things are never just negative or just positive.** The goal is to let feelings flow through you, helping you to know yourself, and to make the mind a vehicle, not the driver. Having an attitude of gratitude helps significantly, as it gives you a perspective of where it is you actually are, as well as increases the level of your "happy" hormone.

Guidelines

☼ **Evaluate your habits.** Write down your everyday routines: from when you wake up, to the time you go to bed. Look at the ones that are tying you down and keeping you stuck. Research ways how you can change them so that your day becomes more enjoyable and more productive. You don't necessarily need to do more, do a little bit better and act more deliberately

☼ **Change your habits gradually.** When you try to do too much at once, it is usually not sustainable. Change one habit and when it becomes easy and automated, change another.

☼ **Watch your inner voice.** When you speak about/to yourself, speak kindly. Give yourself encouragement, especially when you're having a bad day.

☼ **Be mindful of what you are reading, listening to, and watching.** Let it be uplifting, educational, and inspirational.

12.
CHOOSING A HOSPITABLE ENVIRONMENT

"It's inevitable your environment will influence what you do"

Duncan Sheik

The environment you live and spend most of your time in is extremely important to the way you feel. And the way you feel will have a big impact on your motivation, which will affect your decisions and determine how quickly you progress. Choose an environment that feels safe and cosy. Spend most of your time in places that have good energy. Make your home and workplace an environment you actually like being in. Making it useful, modern, and trendy is fine, but it needs to feel homely, it needs to feel like it's nurturing your soul, and that it is inviting. **It also needs to be supportive of what it is you are trying to achieve.** If the center stage of your home is a widescreen TV with surround sound, you are not likely to be spending much quality time with your partner or family.

If your home is designed to be a space where you escape, focusing only on eating, lying on the couch, and tuning out to a Netflix binge, you are less likely to ever start becoming motivated enough to start following your dreams and doing something to actually make things happen. It's great to have a space where you can relax, but it is as important to have a special place where you can create, to have a corner that sparks your imagination by being surrounded by pictures, sounds, fragrances, and tools to help you start developing the skills you might need. You are far more likely to go into a room or corner that is beckoning you to do that little bit to take the next step towards a future you'll love.

I have two desks in my home. One is just for writing, the other is for drawing and painting and I love spending time behind both. I rarely spend time on my couch, I do not own a TV and that is not because I can't afford it, but because it bores and numbs me. My life has become much too exciting and the things I want to learn and create are vast, so having someone else choose what I spend hour after hour staring at, is not appealing to me. I do watch the occasional movie or program, but in the last few years, this is mostly something that can open my mind further, something I can learn from, or work through whatever I'm stuck on at the time. It didn't use to be like this though, I was a movie addict and I would spend half of my day at my job and the other half in front of the TV, trying to block out my own life by watching someone else's through a screen.

The environment you work in – regardless if you work from home or not – should have enough fresh air and light, it should be uplifting and the furthest from dull you can get. Of course, some people can be productive in a boring environment, but your imagination cannot thrive well in it. **Your environment alone should inspire you,** you shouldn't be working extra to get inspired, as you need your energy for other things. Your working space also needs to be clutter-free, but not sterile.

Another thing to consider if you are working seated most of the time is the shape of your chair and the way you are sitting. It is very important that you get up every so often and stretch or even do some light exercise. You can't focus if you're hurting, and sitting down for a long time can sometimes result in spine deterioration or herniated disks. So taking care of your body is extremely important. Considering what you eat, how you sit, and how often you move as well.

Spending time in nature is something else you should consider doing often. **Nature heals, brings about inspiration, and is our true home.** Sunlight, fresh air, soil, and natural bodies of water, are all elements that bring us back into harmony. Spending as much time as you can in nature brings you out of bad days or helps you get in touch with your feelings. Connecting with nature also helps you connect with your true self.

Guidelines

☼ **Make the place where you work, create or do research pleasant to be in.** This is different for each person, but surround yourself with things that lift your spirit and help you stay motivated. These can be pictures, music, colours, affirmations, etc. Have the things that you need around your person, and try to avoid clutter.

☼ **Make it a rule to do some light exercise or stretching once in a while** if you are seated a lot of the time. Be sure to exercise regularly to keep your spine healthy. You can't concentrate if you're in pain or are feeling down, so make an effort to move frequently, eat healthily and get out into fresh air often.

13.
CHOOSING YOUR TRIBE

"Keep your face always toward the sunshine and shadows will fall behind you."

Walt Whitman

If you want to live your dream life, you need to consider unhealthy relationships you might have with some people, which may be a major contributor to what is holding you back. I do not believe in blocking people from your life just because they annoy you. I also know that staying in a relationship can often bring great healing and growth. But if someone is doing you harm, is exploiting you, or making you do things you don't want to be doing, that person does not belong in your life unless it's to teach you how to set boundaries and say no. Breaking away from people who are causing you harm, be it physical or mental, is always devastating at first, but when the energetic link is broken and gradually fades away, only then do you begin to realize how much easier life can be. It's good to stick with someone if you're trying to work things out and they are cooperating, or at least making an effort to. But it is always wise to let go, or to choose minimal contact if this person is keeping you stuck in your old patterns, and keeps dragging you back each time you try to move forward.

When is it a good idea to stay and when to leave? If your gut is telling you they are not meant to be in your life, that is different from your heart or mind telling you to let them stay. **Your gut feeling is always right, you just need to acknowledge it.** The feeling you get may be similar to running away from a house that is on fire. It may be your home, but you know it is dangerous to stay there, even though you might have spent many happy years in it. An important thing to remember with people, as well as fires, is where there is smoke, there is usually trouble.

If someone is showing you traits of themselves you don't like, you can be sure they won't change simply because you have entered their life. The only time a person changes is either when something tragic or significant happens to them, or when they themselves want to change of their own accord. And even then it takes time and patience and a lot of communication. Any relationship - be it romance, business, or friendship - that shows too much devotion and promises things lightly in the beginning stages, should be looked at twice and with a cool head. Letting your gut feeling lead your decisions regarding moving forward with this person, would be even better.

Connecting with people on a similar path to yours is very important. Especially when you feel afraid to take the first step into a new (ad)venture. They have already taken it and see a little further down the road from you, being able to explain what it can look like. Just avoid speaking about your plans with individuals that are negative in their thinking and make everything look almost impossible. Rather choose talking to people who recognize that while not everything is easy, things can be overcome with a little bit of effort and some focus-driven planning. Try being brave and reaching out to people you don't know, be it on social media, in your neighborhood, on the phone, or via email. Some may indeed reject you, but then there are those who will gladly give you advice and talk about the road they have traveled.

Find your tribe and don't rely only on the people you already know to accept what you are doing or to support you in doing it. It's fantastic if they do but if they don't, find people who will. This will give you strength and access to answers and solutions. Your tribe is your support system, your source of inspiration. You have every right to choose the people you want in your life and you also have the right to let them go if their company proves to be destructive to you and your path. Respect, support, truthfulness, and kindness are what you deserve each and every time.

Guidelines

- **Find people who are at least one step ahead of you and connect with them.** Either in person, over emails, in different groups on social media, or in seminars and lectures. Make an effort to find support and guidance, especially in times when you might feel stuck.

- **Do your best to distance yourself from negative energy.** Either by not sharing certain information or by setting boundaries. Sometimes it is better to give some relationships a break to see if this person is really whom you want in your life. Getting help from a professional therapist to help you with difficult relationships is always a good idea too.

14.
OVERCOMING HIDDEN ADDICTIONS

"Passion creates, addiction consumes."

Gabor Maté

Losing touch with yourself and your dreams, trauma, limiting beliefs, and perpetual boredom are some of the main things that evoke addictions. It is not your fault they come about, **but it is only you who can do something about them.** And you can, even though you might think you can't, hoping you might be rescued by someone else. Addictions have many faces, from using drugs to overeating, procrastinating, under or oversleeping, or staring into a screen all day, scrolling away. Unfortunately, many people don't realize they are addicted. They have an unhealthy routine they don't believe they can break. Going to school or work, coming home, playing video games or cleaning obsessively, scrolling through the phone, eating unhealthy food, watching TV, going to bed, and then doing it all over again the next day. Nothing uplifting, nothing creative, and nothing to assist their growth or make their life full. It can all become a vicious cycle, which is hard to break. And even though it seems like you are doing something, you really are just waiting for the day to go by. Granted, perhaps you can't be bothered to do something else but if you want things to change in your life, the only thing that is going to bring it about is doing things differently and actually being present.

It is easy to grab for that remote, but do you think that when you are on your death bed, you'll be wishing you had watched more television? It doesn't happen. It is possible to put a little effort into things you know will make you feel better, things that will slowly make your days astounding. Yes, things may not always go to plan, but imagine being on the verge of giving up, and some major breakthrough happened. And everything gets turned around, giving you a wonderful life, exploring, creating, being able to enjoy your surroundings, and living your dream. Wouldn't it be worth it? What if the additional effort you put into changing your everyday routine becomes a lot easier with time, and the benefits it brings are life-changing? Wouldn't you give it a go and try to stick with it for a while to see if it's actually working?

The reason people can easily get addicted to things that make the pain of their current reality go away, is they imagine change is impossible or extremely difficult, or that they are somehow not deserving of a better life. They may be afraid people around them are going to get upset, that they might lose friends and others close to them. Yes, indeed, the people they care about might not be on board and some might even fall away, but this is only temporary. **Those that oppose you, come around when they see you can't be manipulated** and mean to follow through with your plans. And even if some people do fall away, you will probably meet new ones and they might become better friends, whom you have more in common with.

Being afraid of being alone is another trigger that could get you hooked on things that might later need unhooking. Being alone usually brings up certain emotions you were trying to prevent from surfacing. Many people I know are literally addicted to having company all the time. They absolutely cannot spend any time alone and are mortifyingly miserable if a single day goes by without human contact. If they are alone, these people are usually talking to someone on their phone or texting.

Being alone sometimes means facing your feelings and the reality you are currently living in. And that is often very painful. Although it might not be what you want, it is only temporary and can be changed. Another thing that is good to have in mind is that wanting to create something might mean spending a chunk of time on it by yourself. Distractions may keep you from achieving what it is you've set yourself to achieve. So alone time does not necessarily mean lonely time. Quite the contrary. Alone time might often prove to be growth time, getting in touch with who you are time, and finding out what the heck it is that you want time.

Guidelines

☼ **Be as truthful as you can about the unhealthy habits that you keep repeating.** Please be gentle with yourself and encourage yourself to have a go at something different to change your situation. Get help if you are able to, with the things that seem too hard.

☼ **Look at the things that are keeping you detached from your feelings.** See if there is something you usually go for when you feel uncomfortable. Rather than trying to change the habit, try tapping into the feeling underneath. Feel it in the body and let it go. It will not feel uncomfortable for long, but it will release the urge to reach for something unhealthy or addicting.

15.
SETTING A LOOSE GOAL

"Set your goals high enough to inspire you and low enough to encourage you"

Author unknown

When you are embarking on a completely new quest, you are literally stepping into darkness. Setting an end goal is crucial to knowing what it is you want to take your first steps toward. Setting a single daily goal is just as important. When you have actually set an end goal for yourself and know what you want it to look like, then comes the right time of breaking it into small steps. And when you get a gut feeling to adjust your direction, it's good to act upon it.

The quickest and most effective way I have found for setting short-term goals is by thinking backwards. Say you want to live in your own house sometime in the future. How big is it going to be, what is it going to be made of, how much land is it going to stand on, is it going to have a shed, a fence, solar panels, a cellar..? Take into account as many things as you can, research what it means to build or renovate a home, how much money is needed for the actual material, labour, taxes, and so on. Look at what is available out there. Go and look at houses or properties just for fun, to get into the feel of it. Talk to friends that have bought a home or to real estate agents, builders, look online... Get an actual (even if not precise) idea of the amount of money you will need and the time you'll need to carry out your plan.

Then comes the next step. Thinking of different ways to make the money. Perhaps you could change your job or start a side hustle. Perhaps you could sell things you don't need or invest the money you have. Perhaps borrowing it or taking a loan is an option. What would that entail? Maybe you could even begin your own business that you have wanted to do all along. Write down all of the ways – even if they seem impossible – that you could acquire the money and do it in a relaxed way, so as not to get overwhelmed. And then **choose one way that seems to be the most doable at this moment in time.** And break that down. Say you're good at sewing and you want to make some money selling tote bags. See what you would need to do that. Where can you sell them? Should you open an Etsy shop or sell them in your community? Where could you do that and which people can you contact to help you? What are the nearest and most reliable suppliers of materials? And when you have accomplished that, get to the next thing you could do. You get the picture, don't you?

There are multiple micro steps you can take to slowly get to where you're going. It might seem like a lot, but the good thing is that you don't have to do it all at once, just one thing at a time. This is how it then becomes possible. Another way to go about it is to write your goal on a piece of paper and around it write anything you can think of that you need to do or change to reach it. For example, you might need to get up earlier, you might have to borrow money or save some, you might have to create a web page, you might need to start meditating to become more focused, etc. Then slowly work on each thing you have written down, one by one. You will see that you work through them faster than you imagined you would.

The next step to take can come to you in the form of an idea, a thing that pops up while browsing the internet, something you might hear, or sometimes it even comes to you in a dream. Just be open to it, and keep on researching and trying to figure it out. This journey looks more like feeling for the right turn and changing course if need be, rather than setting your course in stone and sticking to it no matter what. It is very important to have a plan and an end goal. But the short-term goals – the individual steps – might need to be adjusted as you go. Some you'll find will sort of work, and others may just be a waste of time. But then there will be those that will boost you five steps ahead.

Learn to be flexible. This too takes practice. When I started out, I had a plan to work on three things. And along the way, I realized that these three things were just in the way of something I had wanted for a long time. But by working on them, I had learned new skills I would need to achieve my true goal. So I stopped multitasking and started focusing on one thing at a time. The things I omitted have yet to be missed, and the ones that stayed, have been much more enjoyable because I know I'm taking a shortcut, to where I want to be. And even though it might be hard from time to time, I am much more motivated to keep working on what has to be done, to get to the next step.

Many people give up when the new thing they try doesn't work the way they imagined it would. And the thing they thought they wanted, might not be it at all. **You don't need to know exactly what you want to be doing with your life.** Some people know exactly what they want, but most of us only have an idea. We try to mimic what we see someone else doing and/or having. We think the person we are observing feels the way we want to be feeling, but of course, you can never know what the other person is actually going through. You really don't have to have it all worked out. You just need to decide what your next step is and take it. Yes, it does require planning and thinking, but at least you're not thinking about scary things.

Believe me, **you become energized and excited about your life when you start planning practical steps forward.** Of course, there do come days when fear creeps back in. But if you train your mind to look in the direction you want to be going, it should be a momentary thing and should not last for long. And when you get a positive experience, you have a good memory to lean on should the wind of fear decide to blow in your direction.

Guidelines

☼ **Set a long-term goal, but focus on the short-term ones.** They are the ones that will get you there eventually. Make everyday plans and try and accomplish one thing per day in the beginning. More than that is for days when you have a lot of motivation and energy and when you develop more self-discipline and more trust in your abilities. You'll get there, just keep it steady.

☼ **Think backwards.** Write down individual steps to take from your end goal to the present moment. Then take the first step.

16.
TAKING SMALL STEPS

"Action is the foundational key to all success"

Pablo Picasso

Steps are meant to be taken, turns are meant to be mastered and bridges are meant to be crossed. **So if you wish to get somewhere else than where you are now, take action.** Not only think, not only plan but do. Knowing what to do is not as important as dipping your toe in the water and trying things out. By doing things instead of just wishing you could, you build a powerhouse of trust in yourself. You also have a tremendously richer life. Doing instead of thinking of doing is what brings you joy and fulfillment. Doing something may sometimes seem impossible, but this is true only when you imagine the thing you are trying to do, is impossible. So think of something that is less impossible. Is there a step you could take now that could lead in that direction eventually?

I love the analogy of the bicycle: **for the bicycle to be able to move, you are the one who needs to keep moving.** Same as with making progress in anything. So it really doesn't matter if you're not sure what to do, just try something you think might work. The energy you put into things always brings you somewhere, one way or the other.

Sometimes change seems exciting. There might even be a sense of easiness about it. A feeling that you just do what must be done and the results are there in no time. Unfortunately, we often forget that everything in life usually takes time. It also takes a certain amount of dedication and motivation. It most certainly takes a substantial amount of action over time. And the realization that we might have more work cut out for us than we imagined, could possibly throw us off track.

Many people stop trying soon after the "honeymoon" phase. When the adrenaline rush from making the first step subsides, and you are left with the overwhelming feeling of not being good enough to finish what you have started, or to carry it out to a satisfying result. It may even seem you are never going to get there. The initial excitement may easily turn into a disappointment because of all the new things you have to learn, all of the hurdles you have to climb over, and because of the fear of possibly being left behind.

So why is that? Well, **trying to do too much in one go will often kill the motivation and excitement.** That's why focusing on just the next step in front of us is so important. This takes away the fear and obtaining your goal seem more manageable.

Taking small steps will bring you to the top of the mountain, from which you will be able to see your way ahead. **By taking small steps, you can avoid making big mistakes.** There is less collateral damage if the decision you made proves to be the wrong one. It is also easier to tweak your plan of action or look for the right assistance.

The best thing you can do when you feel overwhelmed is to think of just one small, easy thing you can do. This could look something like taking a walk outside if you are feeling anxious or calling someone to ask for advice. You could stop to reevaluate your plan of action, or perhaps repeat affirmations to get motivated if you're the type of person that benefits from them. Perhaps you find you need rest or a change of scenery to get inspired. A seminar or book may get you going again. It really doesn't matter what you do, as long as it is not a distraction that could bring you to a standstill.

Guidelines

- ☼ **Plan big, act small.** Don't try to accomplish a lot at once. Complete one task, and then move on to the next. Long to-do lists are not sustainable. And they may take away your motivation. So make everyday plans and make a single thing a priority.

- ☼ **Keep going no matter what.** When things become overwhelming, stop, take care of your needs, and then have another go. There is nothing better than something coming to fruition after you almost thought of giving up.

17.
DOING YOUR BEST TO STAY MOTIVATED

"You are braver than you believe, stronger than you seem and smarter than you think."

Christopher Robin

On the road to the new you, there are bound to be times that could bring you down. Being unmotivated and discouraged, you can't do anything other than stand still and think about all of the things that are not going right for you. The most difficult thing is to talk yourself into doing something when you absolutely don't want to. Especially if you have a project that you know will take a long time and is not particularly pleasant, but has to be done. This requires making adjustments.

One of these adjustments is **keeping yourself motivated often.** You can't stay motivated all of the time, but finding out what can help you get back on track is a really good idea. Here are some hacks you can try to stay motivated instead of depressed:

☼ Doing a dopamine detox

Dopamine is a hormone in your body that is a pleasure hormone. The more of it there is in your blood, the less you feel like doing anything. Playing video games, watching TV, constant listening to music, internet browsing, collecting likes on social media, constant talking or texting on your phone, and similar everyday activities that make you feel better for a while, will significantly elevate the dopamine in your blood, especially if repeated every day. A result of this elevation is that everything else will seem uninteresting. And I don't mean just a bit but to the point, you won't feel like doing them at all. Dopamine is a very addictive hormone and with a lot of it floating about, it will be very difficult to sit down and concentrate on working on something that will improve the quality of your life.

A dopamine detox would require you to stop all of the activities mentioned above, for a day or more. It is not as hard as it sounds. If this frightens you, just start by eliminating these things for a couple of hours. And then a whole day and then perhaps a whole weekend. You cannot believe the motivation that comes after a dopamine detox. What you are allowed to do on those days is write, draw or create other things, go for walks, exercise, read things that are educational, clean, dance, meditate, garden, and anything similar. Do things that are not passive, but those where you are present, where you have to be engaged and that don't involve screens or similar technology. Something that occupies the creative part of you or calms you down. Working on your projects and doing everyday tasks becomes a whole lot easier after a dopamine detox, and you also feel much more like doing them.

☼ Spending as much time outside as you can

Best in nature, in mild sunlight, and clean air. Make it your everyday task to spend at least one hour a day outside and that's on a bad day. If it's sunny and warm, longer - preferably most of the day. If you can do your work outside, do it outside. Spending that much time away from the comforting embrace of four walls may prove very challenging for some, especially in winter or on rainy days. Having a dog that you have to take walkies twice a day is good motivation. What can make this task pleasurable is making an effort to observe your surroundings. Use all of your senses and breathe deeply. Watching the world through a screen or out of a car is nothing compared to actually tuning in to the world around you physically. You become much more grounded and calm. Especially if you're out in Nature.

☼ Moving

Even when you don't feel like it. I'm not saying to do a full-on exercise regime every day. Just move in any way that feels nice. But do it regularly every day. If you have been physically inactive for a long time, start by doing little things that you can easily do without any special effort. Things like getting up from a chair a couple of times in a row, going for a walk, taking the stairs, or doing some light stretching in your bed every morning. If your body aches all over or you have a little too much weight on you, you might feel better moving in water, sitting, or lying down.

Use your imagination and move intentionally every single day. Physical labour doesn't count. What I mean by moving is training your mind as well as your body to start liking movement again. If you do it regularly in very small amounts, it will start getting to be enjoyable and you'll want to do it more often. This has a direct impact on your mood as well. Our bodies were designed to move most of the day and they start deteriorating by being made to sit still for long periods. Your everyday exercise should be something you enjoy doing a lot. If you don't know what that is, find out by trying different things.

☼ **Eating a healthy diet.**

It is not a coincidence that a standard American diet is called a SAD diet. The kind of diet that lacks fruits and vegetables, contains a lot of refined sugar and a lot of animal protein, saturated fats, is processed and canned, can bring about not only many diseases but also depression and lethargy. Food that is difficult to digest will make you sleepy and will lower your motivation to do anything. Being mindful of what you feed your body will greatly result in more energy and more focus, as well as a lighter mood and outlook on life.

18.

SAVING YOURSELF

"*No one is coming to save you, there is no such thing as a hero, there is only you deciding that you are worthy.*"

Marine Ashnalikyan

You are the only person who knows what kind of life you are meant to be living. No one else knows that, because it is felt, not so much seen. You get one shot at this life (regardless of whether you believe there is a next one). Please take it. **Take as many shots at happiness as you need until it becomes your new normal.** Whether you think you are good enough or if you feel you aren't, have a go. There is always a way if you dare to glance in other directions and there is always assistance if you learn to express what you need help with.

However, relying on others to make your life better is not fair. And there is usually never happiness in it. Demanding something of someone else, which you are capable of doing yourself, is a form of abuse (if you are an adult). You are able to save yourself. You may not have the tools to do it yet, but there are tools out there. Everywhere in fact. **All it takes is your willingness to look around and learn.** Thinking you can't do it doesn't make it true. Believing you will fail is just an old belief that is fueled by fear.

Anyone can become good at whatever it is they are practicing every day, even if only little by little. The speed at which you learn is up to you, but every time you decide to stand still, you are robbing yourself of new opportunities. **Standing still is beneficial only when you are reflecting or resting.** The only limitation you have is your own beliefs, which could be guiding you to failure if they are not supportive of your development. If you believe you can't make friends, you are probably not looking to be around people or when you are, you might sit in a corner thinking to yourself: "see, I can't make friends, I'm just not good enough". Coaxing your thoughts into "there are so many people here, I am bound to find someone to connect with", will make you more approachable, even if you might be shy at first. The truth is that you can do this. It might seem scary, yes, but you have the capability to save yourself from misery and an unfulfilled future. **Take small steps and breathe.** Research, learn. Take small amounts of action and you shall succeed. Sticking to it consistently will prove there is a better life for you and that you are the one creating it.

Something you might consider taking a look at is whether or not you actually need to be saved. Are you really in a situation you have to move away from, or is it your attitude that needs to be altered? Sometimes it's our mind that keeps us stuck and changing our perspective might be enough. It might not, but if you aren't sure, it certainly requires looking into. And if you do need to be saved, what is it that you need to be saved from? Is it your procrastination or outer circumstances? Is it your addiction or perhaps an unhealthy relationship? Is it your habits or old beliefs?

Whatever it is you need or don't need saving from, know

that **you are your own hero** and you don't need to spend precious time waiting for someone else to come and change your life. Begin by believing you have the capacity to make decisions, take steps, get the help you need, and become the hero you have always dreamed would eventually come to your rescue.

Guidelines

- ☼ **Firstly, check if you actually need to be saved.** Are you in a situation you want to get away from or does it need to be tweaked a little? What is it that you can do, even if at first it seems like you can't do much? If you are in a situation you need to get out of, do your research and plan steps towards that. There is always something you can do, even if it means changing your attitude towards it or towards yourself.

- ☼ **Take everyday shots at happiness.** Write down all of the things that make you happy and do one a day. Don't wait for others to bring joy into your life, attract it by doing at least one thing to nurture your soul each day.

19.
LETTING GO

"Anything you can't control is teaching you how to let go."

Jackson Kiddard

How do you turn your life around? You don't. Life is turning on its own. Your job is to follow, be alert, let go when necessary, jump over, crawl under and then go with the flow again. Life is constantly changing, moving, bringing you new experiences. **Your task is not to force things to happen but to stop pushing against what is.** When uncomfortable things happen, they happen either because your thoughts and beliefs have brought you to them, or because there is some learning for you to do. Feeling uncomfortable feelings coincides with this. We are afraid of uncomfortable feelings because we associate them with being told off, punished, neglected, or not loved. We often imagine they will never end. But they do if we let them be felt. They pass and new, better ones emerge when you can see what it is they are trying to show you. That could take a minute, a day, or a month, depending mostly on your openness to look, feel and investigate.

Personally, learning to let go is the hardest thing I've had to do in my life and I'm still finding deeper and deeper layers of it being revealed. Letting go seems scary, it seems like you're allowing things to be wrong, and it feels like you are giving up on your dream. It often feels like giving in. It seems like saying yes to more problems and giving value to the ones that already seem intolerable.

But that is not what it is. **Letting go actually frees you from**

controlling things and losing energy this way. It's scary simply because you imagine a flood of the same or worse being released if you focus on other things that might serve your progress better. But that never happens. **The only sure thing in life is that things change all the time.** First, there is an illusion of chaos, where it looks like things might fall apart, but then a new order comes whereas the things that were meant to, change, fall into place, and the things that were not meant for you, fall away. They would anyway, so why bother holding them in place.

Perpetuating the status quo takes a lot of work and energy. It keeps you stuck in the same muddy hole for years, not being able to focus on anything better. We are all being pressured by our family, friends, and society to pull ourselves together and be in control of our lives. But unfortunately, no one really tells us how to do that, never mind why this would be a good thing. **Life isn't just something you stick in a box and take out every so often, it wants to be free, it wants to evolve and change.** By forcing it to be a certain way, you lose yourself in the process and end up feeling like you're living someone else's life. By not living the life you really want, you are going against your nature and end up depressed, sick, or just numb.

Letting go is an art form. It means being alert to what is happening, what certain situations are trying to teach you, and takes having a limber mind. So don't expect the process to be quick, because there's a whole lot of unlearning to do first. It may be challenging and most certainly accompanied by fear in the beginning. But **by letting go of control, you're letting life bring you what you are working towards in the quickest, easiest, and best way possible.** To be able to do this, you need to develop trust that everything is supporting you to get to where you are going, even if it sometimes doesn't seem that way. Without trust, you start taking the reins back again, wanting more and more control, and then it all gets very complicated, difficult, and takes a long time.

Feeling as though things are slipping out of your hands is justified, as they literally are slipping away from your control into their true nature. And that's how things start flowing. **You get to decide what you want, but life gets to decide how it brings you to it.** You just need to be focused on your feelings, opportunities, and your intuition. You also need to take regular action. It takes some time and quite a bit of practice.

Letting go also means living your truth. Everyone has a sense of what that is, but we have been taught to ignore it. Say you are somewhere you'd rather not be, but you feel it's your obligation to be there. That's ignoring your truth. If you were living it, you'd probably get out of there straight away. Being kind to others in the process is a bonus, but **going against what your being wants and needs, is being unkind to yourself.** Many people are afraid to speak the truth and this is a valid fear, as they could be in danger of being rejected. But if you speak and live your truth unapologetically but explain things with kindness, it is, for the most part, accepted very favourably by most people. Or if not, they get used to it eventually.

So look at what it is you need to let go of. Perhaps it's just that one thing that will enable you to proceed. Perhaps you are holding on to the beliefs from your past and perhaps they need to be reevaluated. We often hold onto our feelings, not allowing them to surface and express themselves. You can turn to your body to find out if you are holding onto something that doesn't belong in your life (anymore). Holding on can manifest as anxiety, depression, fatigue, sleepless nights, constipation, holding your breath, trouble concentrating, inner babbling, agitation, and pain, to name a few. Acknowledge you don't need certain things anymore and that your life can be much easier and happier without them. That's the first and the most important step. The rest you will work out in time.

Guidelines

☼ **When push comes to shove, make the necessary steps and then let go.** Let go of expectations of how things are supposed to look, of how quickly they should change, and what other people should be doing. If this is difficult for you, work on your relaxation or take up something new to keep your mind off it. Do your bit and then let Life do the rest. And if it doesn't open, it's not your door (yet).

☼ **Don't force things.** There is a time and place for everything. You don't get to decide when something is going to unfold or in what way. Just like the ocean forms waves, you don't get to decide how these waves are going to look and how big they are going to be. But you can have a heck of a time learning how to surf. Keep it light and always expect a positive outcome. Use tools like affirmations, meditation, gratitude diary... to keep you stable and develop the right mindset.

20.

EPILOGUE

If you have come to a point in your life where you no longer wish to persist in your current way of living, I congratulate you. It may not be always easy, it may sometimes be scary, but Life has your back, if only you decide to live your truth every single day and learn a lot along the way. We were not born into this world to perpetuate someone else's dream, but our own. If this includes others, all the better. But making your life your own and learning to sail your own boat efficiently, will inevitably bring you to a life you won't need a vacation from. Following your dreams is possible even for you. Never stop taking small steps and have faith that all that is happening is there for a reason to give you what you want in the end. You are here to have joy in your life and joy is your true nature. You can do this. **Just breathe.**

www.ingramcontent.com/pod-product-compliance
Lightning Source LLC
Chambersburg PA
CBHW050012230526
45465CB00003BB/1392